E220207133

C000093628

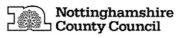Nottinghamshire
County Council

delivered by

Inspire
Culture | Learning | Libraries

I WANT TO BE A
DENTIST

By Joanna Brundle

BookLife
PUBLISHING

©2020
BookLife Publishing Ltd.
King's Lynn
Norfolk PE30 4LS

A catalogue record for this
book is available from the
British Library.

ISBN: 978-1-78637-960-3

Written by:
Joanna Brundle

Edited by:
William Anthony

Designed by:
Dan Scase

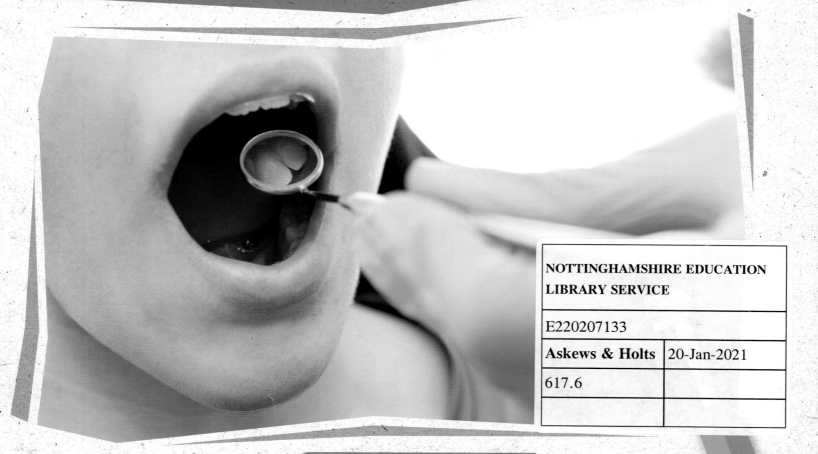

PHOTO CREDITS:
Images are courtesy of Shutterstock.com.
With thanks to Getty Images, Thinkstock Photo and iStockphoto.
Front Cover – LineTale, Irina Tihomirova, Billion Photos, Solis Images, Julia Pankin, Captian'N, matkub2499, ANRproduction, 281441645
4&5 – ONYXprj, michaeljung, MIA Studio. 6&7 – Lighthunter, Rido, Kletr. 8&9 – Ilya Andriyanov, zlikovec. 10&11 – Sunshine Seeds, AS photo
studio. 12&13 – Nadir Keklik. 14&15 – Monkey Business Images, michaeljung. 16&17 – carballo, hightowernrw, FotoDuets, gpointstudio, al7,
Pavel L Photo and Video, baklykovadaria. 18&19 – Mr. Luck. 20&21 – Sunshine Seeds, Loveischiangrai. 22&23 – Littlekidmoment, Ana D.
Vectors throughout: kotoffei

CONTENTS

PAGE 4   **Hello, I'm Dexter!**

PAGE 6   **What Will I Do?**

PAGE 8   **How Will I Help People?**

PAGE 10   **Where Will I Work?**

PAGE 12   **Can I Look around a Dental Surgery?**

PAGE 14   **What Will I Wear?**

PAGE 16   **What Equipment Will I Use?**

PAGE 18   **Let's Look at Our Teeth**

PAGE 20   **Where Could I Work around the World?**

PAGE 22   **How Can We Look after Our Teeth?**

PAGE 24   **Glossary and Index**

Words that look like <u>this</u> can be found in the glossary on page 24.

HELLO, I'M DEXTER!

Hello, I'm Dexter! When I grow up, I want to be a dentist. You could be one too! Let's find out what this job will be like.

I want to be a dentist so that I can help people to look after their teeth and gums. Teeth are very important. We use them for biting and chewing food.

Healthy teeth also give us a great smile!

WHAT WILL I DO?

I will check my <u>patients'</u> teeth for problems. I will also make sure that children's teeth are growing properly. I may even remove <u>decay</u> and fill or repair any damaged teeth.

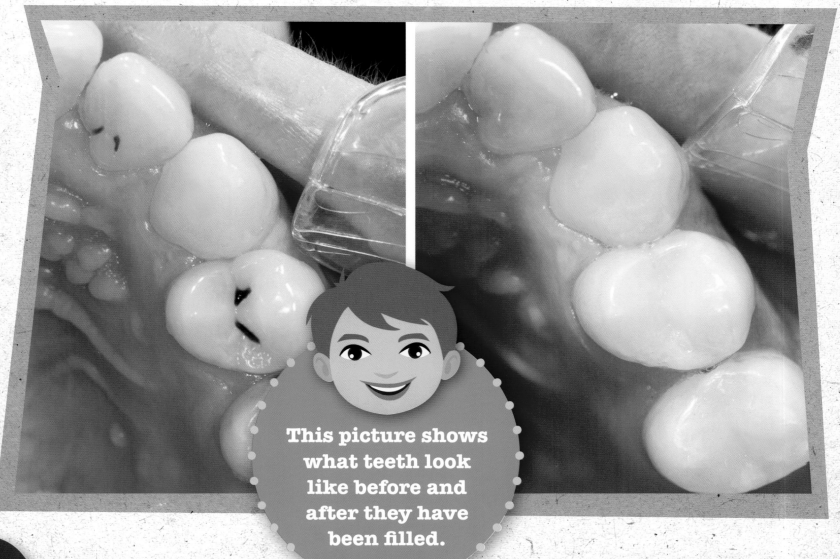

This picture shows what teeth look like before and after they have been filled.

X-rays will help me to look for problems. I might have to take out a tooth or help to straighten a patient's teeth by fitting **braces**.

Braces

X-ray

7

HOW WILL I HELP PEOPLE?

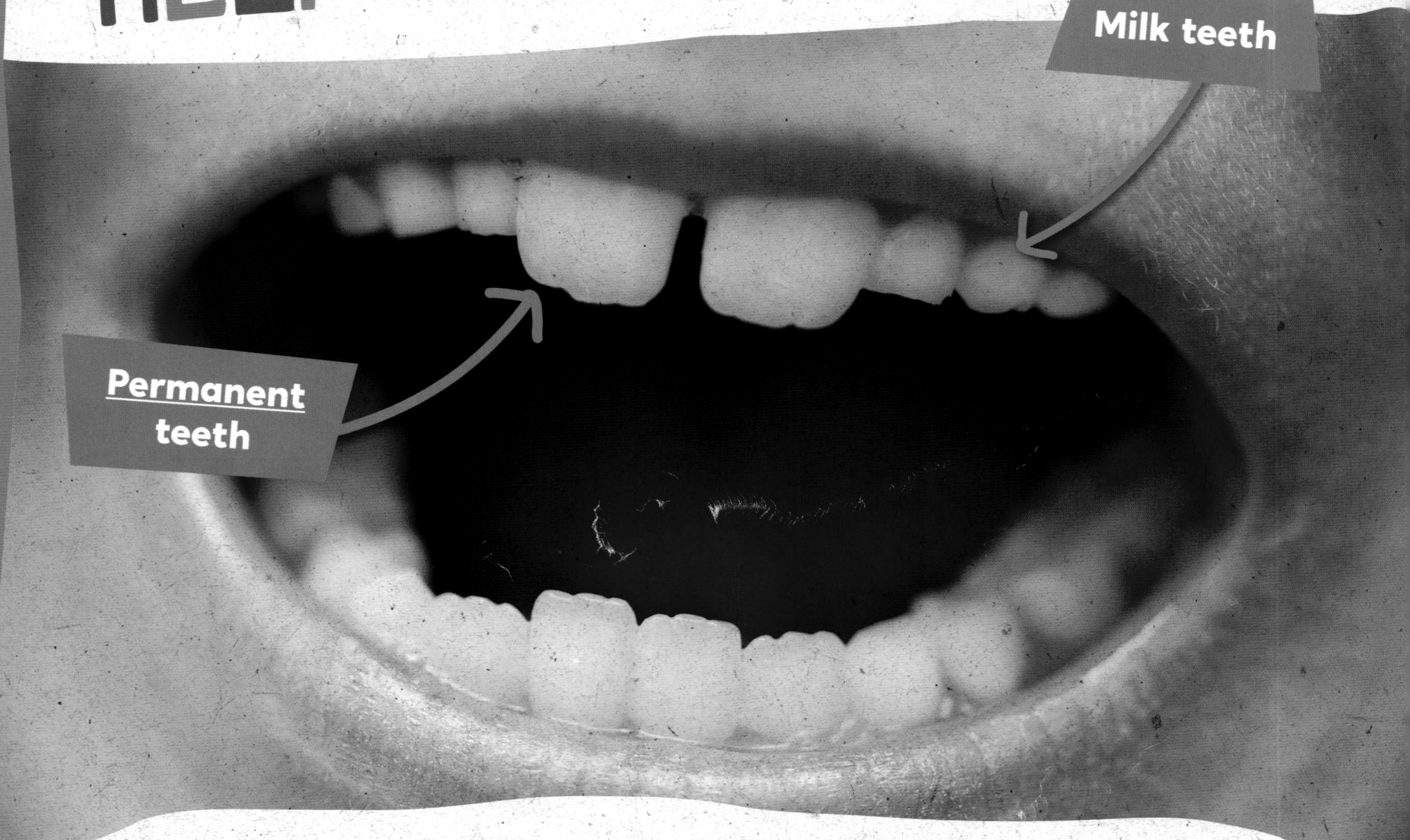

Milk teeth

Permanent teeth

Our first teeth, called milk teeth, fall out and we get a second set. But did you know that this set has to last the rest of our lives? I will help people look after both sets.

I will teach my patients to brush and <u>floss</u> their teeth correctly. It's important to make sure we brush all around and between our teeth.

Some dentists might let you bring a teddy into your appointment. They may give you a sticker or toothbrush after your appointment.

WHERE WILL I WORK?

I may work in a dental surgery. Surgeries are found in cities, towns, villages and even shopping centres and supermarkets.

This is a mobile dental surgery. This means it travels to patients.

I might work in a hospital, helping patients who need operations or other special care. Some patients have to be seen at home if they are elderly or disabled.

Some dentists work in dental schools, teaching other people how to be dentists.

CAN I LOOK AROUND A DENTAL SURGERY?

A light helps the dentist to see into a patient's mouth.

Patients can rinse their teeth at this sink.

The dental assistant uses the equipment kept here.

The dentist's equipment is kept here.

The chair can be moved up or down. The backrest moves forwards and backwards.

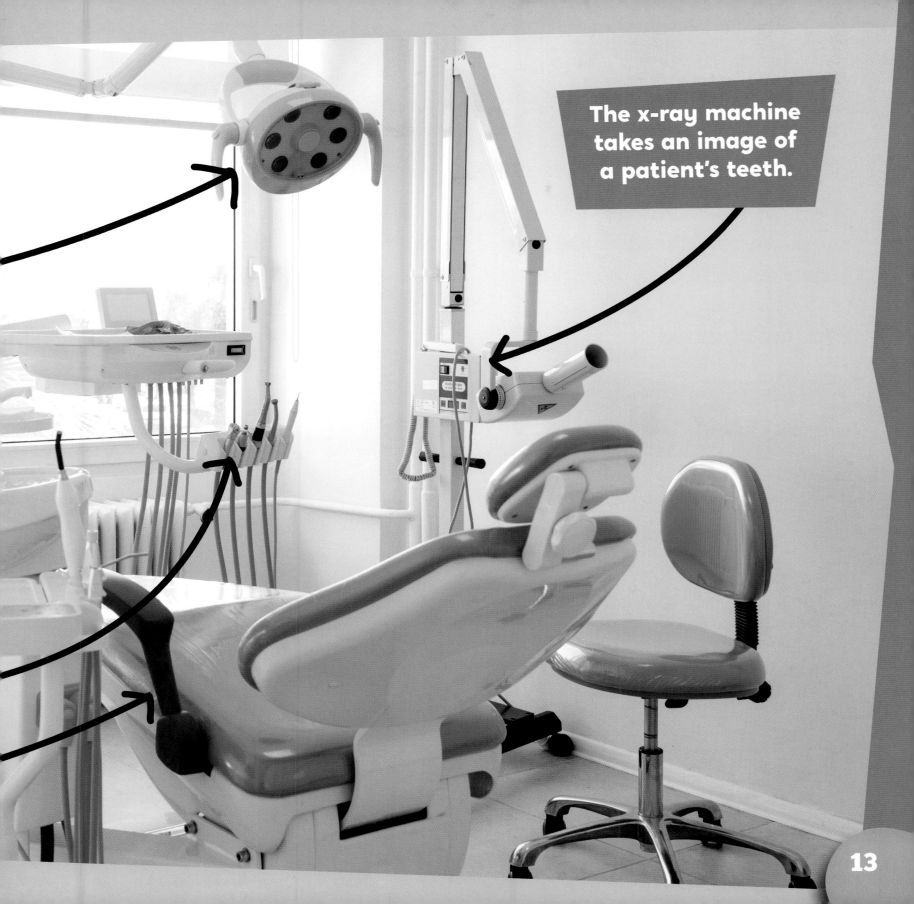

The x-ray machine takes an image of a patient's teeth.

13

WHAT WILL I WEAR?

I might wear clothes called scrubs. These are loose-fitting shirts and trousers that help me move around easily. Some dentists wear a white coat over the top of scrubs or normal clothes.

Scrubs

White coat

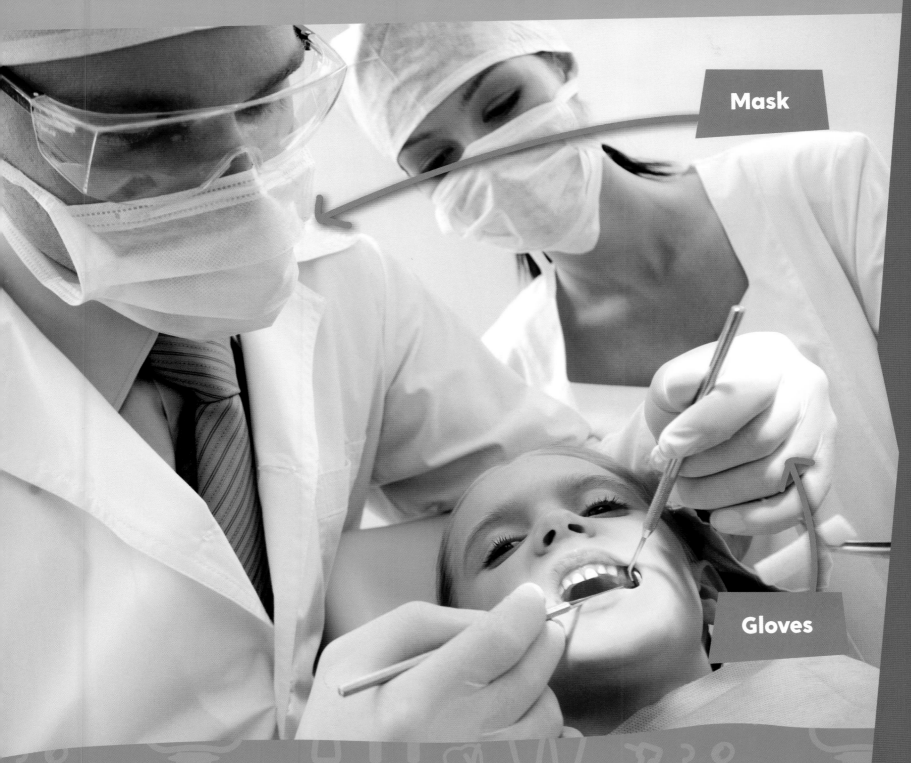

Mask

Gloves

I will wear a cap over my hair, a mask and some gloves to avoid <u>infection</u>. I may also wear goggles to protect my eyes.

WHAT EQUIPMENT WILL I USE?

Let's have a look at some of the equipment I will use.

Mirror – used to look around a patient's mouth

Dental probe – used to check for tooth decay

Drill – used to remove any decay before a tooth is filled

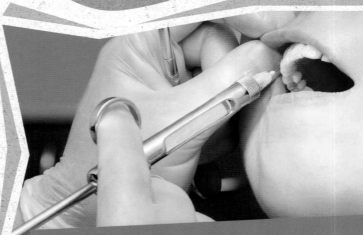

Syringe – used to give an <u>anaesthetic</u>, so that the patient feels no pain

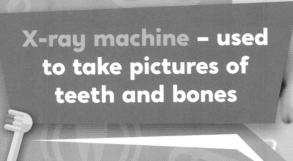

X-ray machine – used to take pictures of teeth and bones

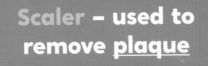

Scaler – used to remove <u>plaque</u>

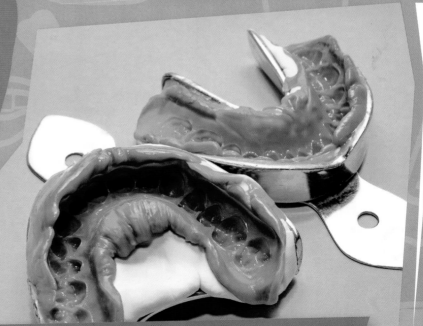

Dental moulds – used to make braces or <u>mouthguards</u>

LET'S LOOK AT OUR TEETH

We have 32 permanent teeth but only 20 milk teeth.

TOP TEETH

BOTTOM TEETH

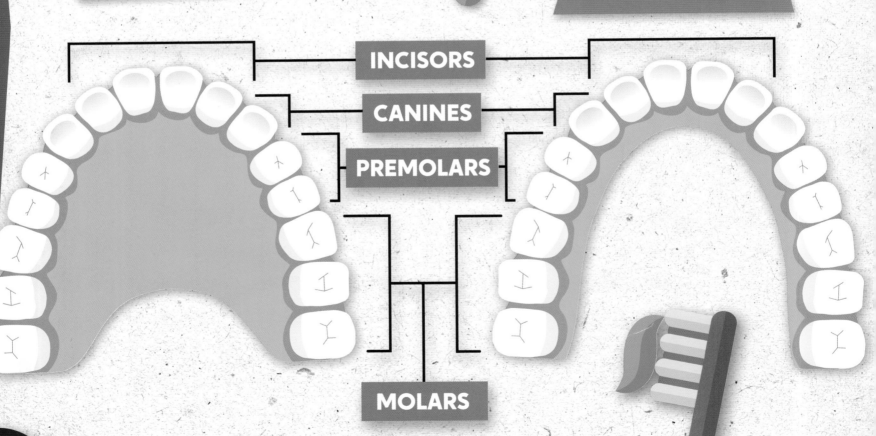

INCISORS

CANINES

PREMOLARS

MOLARS

18

Incisors – Incisors are thin, sharp teeth. They are used for cutting food into small pieces.

Canines – Canines are sharp and pointed. They are used for gripping and tearing food.

Premolars – Premolars have a flat biting surface. They are used for crushing and tearing food.

Molars – Molars are our largest teeth. They are used for grinding, crushing and chewing food.

Roots – Each tooth has a root that holds it in place.

WHERE COULD I WORK AROUND THE WORLD?

Tomorrow Starts Today

Telkom

Impilo Enhle Servicing the community, serving you

Rhiza Mobile Clinic
Mother and Child & Dental Services

PHILIPS IDC Industrial Development Corporation NOZALA TRUST

VISIQ: High quality ultrasound

Some countries have mobile surgeries like this one.

In some countries, there are very few dentists. Many people in these countries may not have access to a dentist at all.

Some dentists work as <u>volunteers</u> in these countries. They treat patients and train new dentists. They also teach people how to care for their teeth and gums.

This volunteer dentist is working at a school in Thailand.

HOW CAN WE LOOK AFTER OUR TEETH?

We need to brush our teeth properly at least twice a day for about two minutes each time. Afterwards, don't rinse – just spit out. Toothpaste contains fluoride, which is something that helps to protect our teeth.

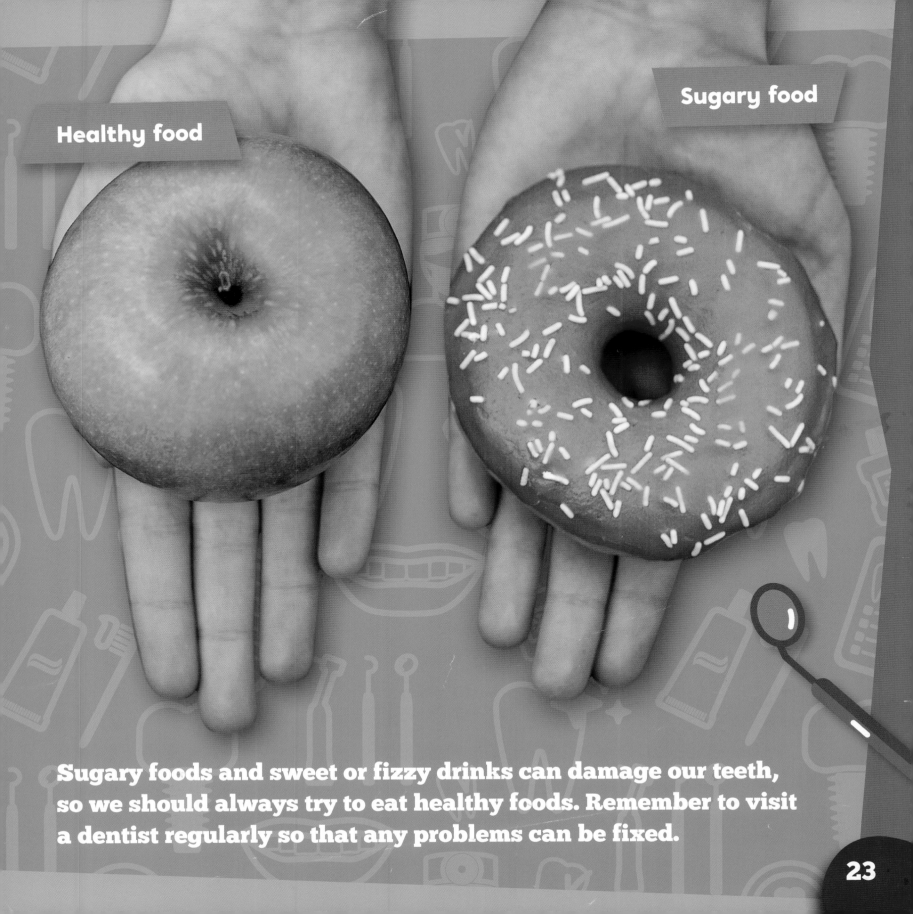

Healthy food

Sugary foods and sweet or fizzy drinks can damage our teeth, so we should always try to eat healthy foods. Remember to visit a dentist regularly so that any problems can be fixed.

GLOSSARY

ANAESTHETIC   a substance put into a patient's body to stop pain

BRACES   devices fitted to crooked teeth to make them straight

DECAY   a rotten part of something

FLOSS   clean between the teeth using a fine, soft thread

INFECTION   illness caused by dirt or microbes getting into the body

MOUTHGUARDS   devices that fit over the teeth and gums to protect them during sport

PATIENTS   people who are given medical care or treatment

PERMANENT   meant to last forever

PLAQUE   a substance containing bacteria (germs) that forms on the teeth, which can damage gums and teeth if it is not removed

VOLUNTEERS   people who work or help others without being paid

X-RAYS   pictures taken by an x-ray machine that show the inside of the body, particularly teeth and bones

INDEX

clothes 14–15

decay 6, 16

dental surgeries 10, 12–13, 20

equipment 12–13, 16–17

fillings 6, 16

gums 5, 21

hospitals 11

teeth

- canines 18–19

- incisors 18–19

- milk 8, 18

- molars 18–19

- permanent 8, 18

- premolars 18–19

volunteers 21

x-rays 7, 13, 17